# TOUGH TRUCKS

# TOYOTA TACOMA

## BY LARRY MACK

TM

BELLWETHER MEDIA • MINNEAPOLIS, MN

TM

Are you ready to take it to the extreme?
Torque books thrust you into the action-packed world
of sports, vehicles, mystery, and adventure. These books may
include dirt, smoke, fire, and dangerous stunts.
**WARNING** read at your own risk.

This edition first published in 2019 by Bellwether Media, Inc.

No part of this publication may be reproduced in whole or in part without written permission of the publisher.
For information regarding permission, write to Bellwether Media, Inc., Attention: Permissions Department,
6012 Blue Circle Drive, Minnetonka, MN 55343.

Library of Congress Cataloging-in-Publication Data

Names: Mack, Larry, author.
Title: Toyota Tacoma / by Larry Mack.
Description: Minneapolis, MN : Bellwether Media, Inc., 2019. | Series:
   Torque: Tough Trucks | Includes bibliographical references and index. |
   Audience: Ages 7-12.
Identifiers: LCCN 2018002186 (print) | LCCN 2018007219 (ebook) | ISBN
   9781626178960 (hardcover : alk. paper)| ISBN 9781681036151 (ebook)
Subjects: LCSH: Tacoma truck–Juvenile literature.
Classification: LCC TL230.5.T68 (ebook) | LCC TL230.5.T68 M33 2019 (print) |
   DDC 629.223/2-dc23
LC record available at https://lccn.loc.gov/2018002186

Editor: Betsy Rathburn     Designer: Josh Brink

Printed in the United States of America, North Mankato, MN.

# TABLE OF CONTENTS

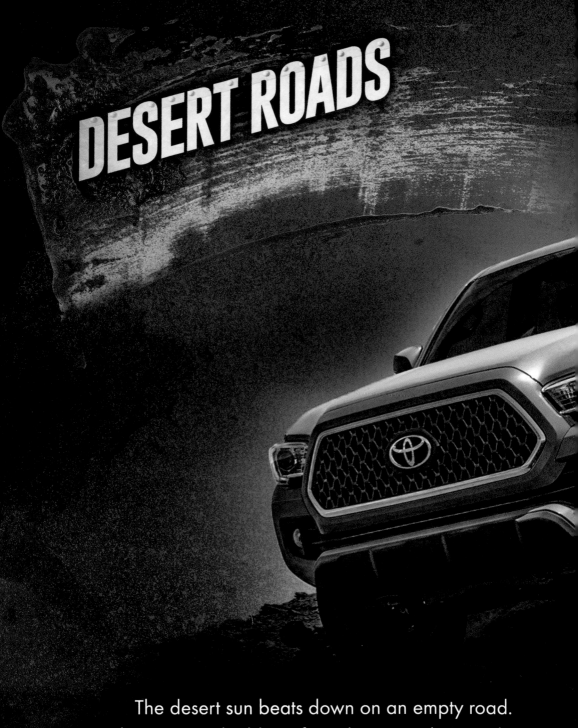

# DESERT ROADS

The desert sun beats down on an empty road. There are no buildings for miles around. Animals keep cool in any shade they can find.

A jackrabbit's ears twitch as a faraway sound grows louder. A pickup truck bursts over a hill in a cloud of dust. The desert heat and sand are no match for the Toyota Tacoma!

The driver slides the truck around a corner. **Four-wheel drive** and tough tires give the Tacoma a good grip on the ground.

Inside, the driver and passenger are safe from the heat. Rocks and hot sand stretch as far as their eyes can see. They know their Tacoma will get them home safely.

# TOYOTA TACOMA HISTORY

In 1926, Japanese businessman Sakichi Toyoda started a company called Toyoda Automatic Loom Works. It built improved **looms** so people could create **textiles** much faster.

**Sakichi Toyoda**

**Toyota AA**

In time, the company started making cars. Its name changed to Toyota Motor Company. Toyota cars and trucks are now sold around the world!

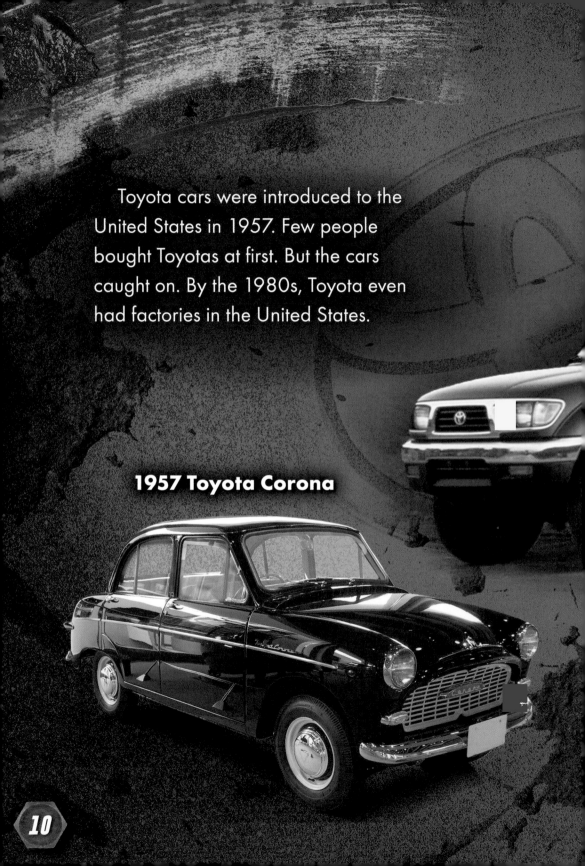

Toyota cars were introduced to the United States in 1957. Few people bought Toyotas at first. But the cars caught on. By the 1980s, Toyota even had factories in the United States.

**1957 Toyota Corona**

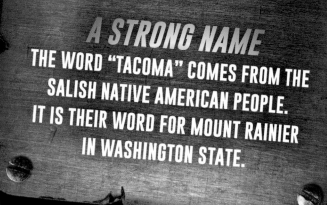

**1995 Toyota Tacoma**

Soon, Toyota wanted to take on American trucks like Ford. They introduced new full-size pickups in 1993. Two years later, the Toyota Tacoma was introduced!

# TOYOTA TACOMA TODAY

Today, the Tacoma is Toyota's most popular pickup. It comes in six different **models**. Each is popular for its safety features and gadgets!

These trucks are known for their comfortable ride and sporty style. They also have **reliable** engines. This makes them a good choice for any driver!

**TAKE YOUR PICK**
SOME TACOMAS ARE AVAILABLE IN AS MANY AS TEN COLORS!

**2016 Toyota Tacoma SR5**

**2016 Toyota Tacoma TRD Sport**

# FEATURES AND TECHNOLOGY

Tacoma owners can choose a **four-cylinder** or six-cylinder engine. The engine gives the truck the power to haul, tow, and handle tough roads.

Some Tacoma pickups have a feature called CRAWL. This controls the brakes and **throttle** while the driver focuses on steering over rough roads!

**3.5L V6 engine**

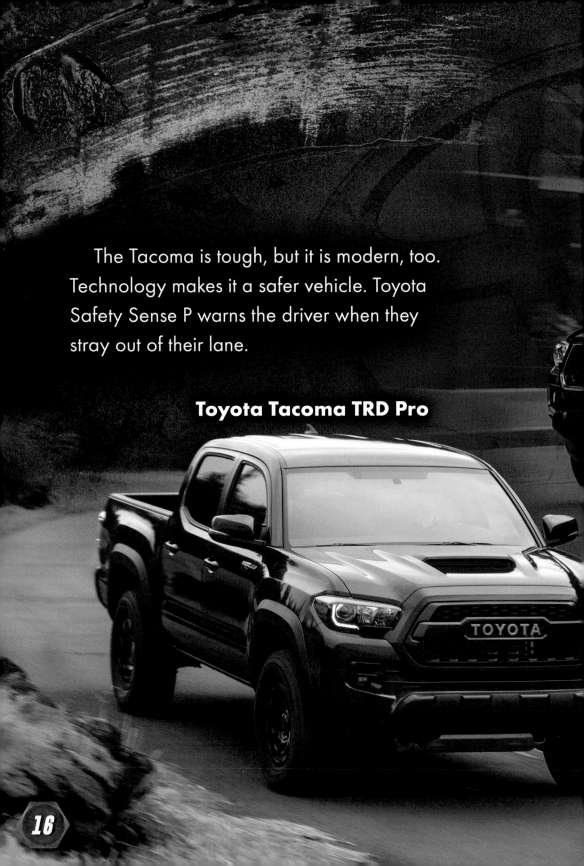

The Tacoma is tough, but it is modern, too. Technology makes it a safer vehicle. Toyota Safety Sense P warns the driver when they stray out of their lane.

**Toyota Tacoma TRD Pro**

# CLIMBING HIGH

HILL START ASSIST IS A TACOMA FEATURE THAT HELPS DRIVERS STAY SAFE ON STEEP ROADS. IT KEEPS THE TRUCK FROM ROLLING BACKWARDS!

The feature also warns the driver if someone steps into the street. It can even set the speed so the driver does not go over the speed limit!

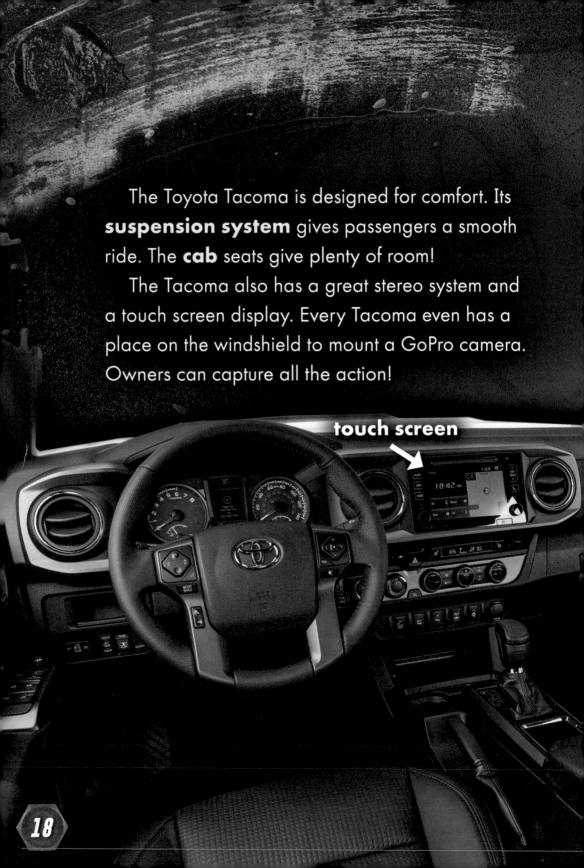

The Toyota Tacoma is designed for comfort. Its **suspension system** gives passengers a smooth ride. The **cab** seats give plenty of room!

The Tacoma also has a great stereo system and a touch screen display. Every Tacoma even has a place on the windshield to mount a GoPro camera. Owners can capture all the action!

**touch screen**

# 2018 TOYOTA TACOMA LIMITED SPECIFICATIONS

| | |
|---|---|
| ENGINE | 3.5L V6 ENGINE |
| HORSEPOWER | 278 HP (207 KILOWATTS) @ 6,000 RPM |
| TORQUE | 265 LB-FT (37 KG-M) @ 4,600 RPM |
| TOWING CAPACITY | UP TO 6,600 POUNDS (2,994 KILOGRAMS) |
| MAXIMUM PAYLOAD | 1,370 POUNDS (621 KILOGRAMS) |
| FUEL ECONOMY | 19 TO 24 MILES PER GALLON |
| CURB WEIGHT | UP TO 4,480 POUNDS (2,032 KILOGRAMS) |
| WHEEL SIZE | 18 INCHES (46 CENTIMETERS) |

# TRUCK OF THE FUTURE

The Toyota Tacoma combines many features pickup fans love. It has a powerful engine that can handle **off-road** fun.

# HOW TO SPOT A TOYOTA TACOMA

**ANGLED HEADLIGHTS**

**SMOOTH LINES**

**SIX-SIDED GRILLE**

The Tacoma is so popular that Toyota may build a **hybrid** version. This is a sure sign the Tacoma will remain Toyota's truck of the future!

# GLOSSARY

**cab**—the area of a pickup where the driver and passengers sit

**four-cylinder**—having four separate cylinders; a cylinder is a chamber in an engine in which fuel is ignited.

**four-wheel drive**—a feature that allows the engine to turn all four of a vehicle's wheels at once

**hybrid**—a vehicle that uses both gasoline and electricity for fuel

**looms**—machines that help create textiles

**models**—specific kinds of trucks

**off-road**—taking place on unpaved roads

**reliable**—trusted to perform well

**suspension system**—a series of springs and shocks that help a truck grip the road

**textiles**—pieces of fabric

**throttle**—a control that sends fuel to an engine to create power

# TO LEARN MORE

## AT THE LIBRARY

Bowman, Chris. *Pickup Trucks*. Minneapolis, Minn.: Bellwether Media, 2018.

Mack, Larry. *Honda Ridgeline*. Minneapolis, Minn.: Bellwether Media, 2019.

Mack, Larry. *Nissan Frontier.* Minneapolis, Minn.: Bellwether Media, 2019.

## ON THE WEB

Learning more about the
Toyota Tacoma is as easy us 1, 2, 3.

1. Go to www.factsurfer.com.

2. Enter "Toyota Tacoma" into the search box.

3. Click the "Surf" button and you will see a list
   of related web sites.

With factsurfer.com, finding more information
is just a click away.

# INDEX